# Sequences

Kay Gardiner and Ann Shayne

INTRODUCTION

I N EARLY 2015, we received an intriguing email from Cecelia Campochiaro, a knitter whose profession in Silicon Valley is to develop finely calibrated machines that inspect computer chips.

Cecelia told us that while seeking "very simple knitting projects" to work on during business travel, she had ended up "unventing" a simple way of knitting in which complex-looking fabrics "just happen." Cecelia had self-published a book about the technique, called *Sequence Knitting*, and she wanted to send us a copy.

We did not say no. As longtime devotees of open-ended techniques—log cabin knitting and freeform colorwork, for example— we were intrigued.

The modesty of Cecelia's email did not prepare us for the incredible volume that arrived on our doorstep a few days later.

The book is akin to a scientific classification of the many knitted fabrics that result from repeating simple knit-and-purl sequences over different multiples of stitches, using various rules of stopping and starting. At 388 pages and four-and-a-half pounds, it is a whopper.

And it has revolutionized the way we think about knitting.

In one sense, however, there is nothing revolutionary about sequence knitting. Cecelia, a scientist by training, has merely identified and described something that occurs in knitting all the time, whether we notice it or not. Lots of familiar stitch patterns fit the definition of sequence knitting: 2×2 ribbing, mistake rib, seed stitch, even lace patterns. Cecelia's book reveals the hidden architecture of knitted fabric and organizes it into something we can do on purpose, thereby creating many new textures of knitted fabric intuitively and without using a chart.

As knitters, we are trained to think of stitch patterns as specific motifs to be learned, practiced, and memorized. (Think of Barbara Walker's legendary stitch dictionaries, and the hundreds of quaintly named patterns in those pages.) With sequence knitting, we suddenly see the rhythms that underlie all textured stitch patterns and how a change of one stitch in either the sequence of knits and purls, or in the number of stitches in the row or round, can completely alter the fabric we produce.

Before *Sequence Knitting*, it had not occurred to us, in our many years of practice, to knit a sequence over a multiple of stitches, either as a one-row pattern or a pattern that continues without a break from the right side to the wrong side of the work, and just

see what happens. We have held the power in our hands and minds all this time, and we have not used it. It's liberating—and empowering. It enables us to buy yarn for its beauty, without knowing exactly what to make with it, and to know for sure that we will be able to turn it into an extraordinary textured fabric.

We were thrilled when Cecelia agreed to collaborate with us on this Field Guide, conceived as an introduction to the four concepts of sequence knitting by way of four clever projects of Cecelia's design. Where *Sequence Knitting* is a deep exploration of those concepts, this Field Guide is a tantalizing taste.

MDK Rule No. 1: Knitting is supposed to be fun.

Sequence knitting is all the things we love: it's relaxing, meditative, with a spark of cleverness to keep us changing things up, experimenting. In a word, fun.

*Kay     Ann*

# FOUR
# BASIC FORMS
## *of*
# SEQUENCE
# KNITTING

T HERE ARE FOUR BASIC KINDS of sequence knitting. These have to do with what happens when you begin a new row. Do you stop the sequence and start it anew on the next row? Or do you let the sequence "turn the corner" at the end of a row and continue uninterrupted on the next row? What about when you knit in the round, or add increases or decreases? Curious and interesting things happen in each and every case.

**1-Row.** The sequence is worked to the end of the row, then begins anew at the beginning of the new row. Every row is the same. The Corrugated Shawl on page 8 includes eight 1-row patterns.

**Serpentine.** The sequence is worked to the end of the row, then the sequence wraps around the edge of the fabric to continue uninterrupted as the new row begins. The rows are often different from each other. The Corrugated Shawl on page 8 includes 8 serpentine patterns.

**Spiral.** The sequence is worked in the round. This takes a sequence into a whole new realm, because the beginning-of-round marker does not interrupt the sequence. Check out the Swirl Hat on page 18.

**Shaped 1-Row.** An increase or decrease at the end of a row throws a sequence into a different pattern. See this idea in action in the Freak Flags on page 24 and the Parallelogram Scarf on page 30.

## *This is our idea of a good time.*

THE BEST WAY TO GET a feel for the way sequence knitting works is to knit a bunch of sequences, one after the other. The single change of a stitch in a sequence can make your fabric utterly different. As much as we have been experimenting with sequences, we are still surprised when this happens.

It's just so cool.

At the conclusion of the Corrugated Shawl, you'll find yourself with a luxurious wrap that contains 16 different sequence stitch patterns. The trick here is to choose smooth, round yarns with excellent stitch definition—sorry, but we're going to steer you away from wildly variegated yarns. You want to see what's going on with the sequences, where the patterns can sometimes be subtle and surprising.

The yarn here, Crave Yarn's dreamy Caravan, is unabashedly luxurious. If you're going to be making a wrap like this, so beautifully simple yet somehow intricate, it feels right to use a special yarn. In our experience, knitting a luxurious yarn is a form of self-care. OK, so it's a form of indulgence too, but if we don't indulge ourselves, who will?

CORRUGATED
SHAWL

## KNITTED MEASUREMENTS
Width: Approx 15" [38 cm]
Length: Approx 78" [198 cm]

## MATERIALS
— Caravan by Crave Yarn [100 g skeins,
  each approx 354 yds (323 m),
  70% superwash fine merino/
  10% camel/ 10% cashmere/
  10% mulberry silk)]: 4 skeins
  Full shawl shown on pages 8–9 and
  12–13 in Authenticity. Swatches
  shown on page 2 in Tilly (brown),
  Franklin (gray), Realm (dark teal),
  Authenticity (cream), and Nuance
  (light teal).
— One pair size US 5 (3.5 mm) needles,
  or size needed to achieve gauge
— Removable stitch marker

## GAUGE
26 sts and 36 rows = 4" (10 cm) over St st

## NOTES
This sampler shawl uses 16 different
sequence-knitting fabrics separated
by spacers of stockinette and reverse
stockinette stitch. The gauge of each
fabric is different, and this, combined
with the natural curl of the stockinette
stitch, creates the corrugated effect.

The pattern is best worked in a luxury
yarn with a clean structure to empha-
size the different textures and make a
luscious fabric.

For the sequence-knitting sections,
the work is done with either the 1-row
method, where a sequence is restarted
and then repeated across the row, or the
serpentine method, where the sequence
continues from row to row.

The stitch count is not changed through-
out the work, and each section is worked
over a multiple of 4 stitches + 2 or 8
stitches + 2. To change the width, add or
subtract stitches in increments of 8.

You will not always be able to work a
complete sequence before the end of the
row. In the case of a partial sequence,
continue to work the leftover stitches in
pattern to the end.

If you use a long-tail cast-on, be sure to
cast on loosely by either using a larger
needle or spacing out the stitches as
they are formed to ensure that the
cast-on edge is not too narrow.

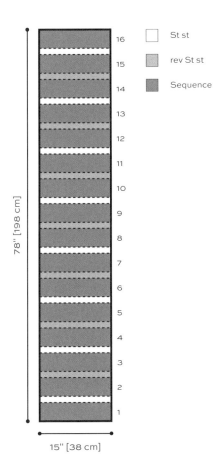

16

15

14

13

12

11

10

9

8

7

6

5

4

3

2

1

☐ St st

▨ rev St st

▨ Sequence

78" [198 cm]

15" [38 cm]

# SHAWL

CO 98 sts and place a marker around the first st. This indicates the beginning of the piece; when the shawl is viewed from the front, this marker will be at the bottom right and will help with counting rows.

Work the sections following the table on page 14. Work each section of sequence knitting for 36 rows, followed by 12 rows of St st or rev St st as indicated; the final section will be worked in sequence knitting.

After the table is complete, BO all sts.

## FINISHING

Weave in ends.

Soak piece in water with a wool wash or shampoo for at least 30 minutes to thoroughly wet the fabric. Rinse and press out the water repeatedly until the water runs clear. Then spin out any remaining water (salad spinners work wonders; or place in a lingerie bag and swing outdoors to shake out water). Lay out the shawl on a flat surface, and pin the 4 corners to the final dimensions. Smooth the shawl, and put pins at the top and bottom of each sequence-knitting section, letting the stockinette edges curl.

## CORRUGATED SHAWL TABLE

\* Work 36 rows of all Sequence Patterns

\*\* Work 12 rows of all Spacer Patterns

| Section No. | Sequence Pattern * | Sequence Method | Row Repeat | Fabric Description | Spacer Pattern ** |
|---|---|---|---|---|---|
| 1 | [k2, p2] | 1-row | 2 | Broken garter | St st |
| 2 | [k2, p2] | serpentine | 4 | 2x2 rib | rev St st |
| 3 | [k3, p1] | 1-row | 2 | Mistake rib | St st |
| 4 | [k4, p4] | 1-row | 2 | Accordion | rev St st |
| 5 | [k4, p4] | serpentine | 4 | Broken welting | St st |
| 6 | [k3, p4, k1] | serpentine | 4 | All over | rev St st |
| 7 | [k5, p3] | 1-row | 2 | Mistake rib | St st |
| 8 | [k5, p3] | serpentine | 4 | All over | rev St st |
| 9 | [k6, p2] | 1-row | 2 | Accordion | St st |
| 10 | [k5, p2, p1] | 1-row | 2 | Mistake rib | rev St st |
| 11 | [k6, p2] | serpentine | 4 | Broken rib | St st |
| 12 | [k3, p2, k3] | serpentine | 4 | All over | rev St st |
| 13 | [k5, p1, k1, p1] | 1-row | 2 | Mistake rib/accordion | St st |
| 14 | [k5, p1, k1, p1] | serpentine | 4 | All over | rev St st |
| 15 | [k2, p1, k1, p2, k1, p1] | 1-row | 2 | Broken garter | St st |
| 16 | [k2, p1, k1, p2, k1, p1] | serpentine | 4 | All over | BO |

SHAWL (OR SCARF)
OF ONE'S OWN

\*     Work __ rows of all Sequence Patterns

\*\*    Work __ rows of all Spacer Patterns

| Section No. | Sequence Pattern * | Sequence Method | Row Repeat | Fabric Description | Spacer Pattern ** |
|---|---|---|---|---|---|
| 1 | | | | | |
| 2 | | | | | |
| 3 | | | | | |
| 4 | | | | | |
| 5 | | | | | |
| 6 | | | | | |
| 7 | | | | | |
| 8 | | | | | |
| 9 | | | | | |
| 10 | | | | | |
| 11 | | | | | |
| 12 | | | | | |
| 13 | | | | | |
| 14 | | | | | |
| 15 | | | | | |
| 16 | | | | | |

The Corrugated Shawl Table at left makes it super easy to see the pattern at a glance; so easy, in fact, that once you've tried it out, you may want to cook up a sequence shawl (or scarf) of your own. We offer this blank table as an enticement.

Find a yarn you love. Remember: Smooth, round yarn shows stitches best; light colors show off the stitchwork most clearly; slow-changing gradients and ombres are fine; wild variegateds are dangerous! Figure out what gauge would create a scarf or shawl at the width you desire, and fill out this chart with your own personal recipe of sequences. You can include spacer patterns (rows of plain stockinette or reverse stockinette) as you like, or not. They give the sequences a bit of elbow room to shine, but they're not required. The odds of this looking cool are very high. We can't wait to see what you create.

# THINGS
# ORGANIZED
# NEATLY

**M**Y GRANDMOTHER'S PANTRY had a row of hooks that had been painted over many times, in creamy white. The hooks were at the eye level of a preschool child, under bracketed shelves that held flour and sugar in glass jars and cookies in packets from the store. From these hooks hung Grandma's saucepans, none of which matched and most of which were dented or scorched. Hanging there in a row, they looked serene and orderly. As a small kid, I would open the pantry door just to look at the saucepans. Then I'd give each one a little shove, and set them all to rocking against the beadboard wall.

I still find great satisfaction in order, in a kitchen drawer or on a museum wall. One of the best gifts I ever received was a copy of the book *How to Wrap Five Eggs*, by Hideyuki Oka. And I can spend hours looking at the Tumblr account Things Organized Neatly, which is full of aesthetically pleasing arrangements of ordinary objects. Who spends their time arranging all of their erasers like a Mondrian painting? I don't know, but I salute these anonymous heroes. I love their work.

—Kay

# SWIRL
# HAT

T RUTH BE TOLD, we like our hats kind of
understated. We also like a hat to be a simple
and entertaining sort of knitting project,
which is where sequence knitting comes in handy.
In this brand of knitting, a hat's textural shifts are
folded into the sequence in a perfectly organic way.

Speaking of organic, the yarn you see here is so
noble, so unpretentious, that Brooke Sinnes, the
yarnmaker who creates it in northern California,
named it Sincere Sheep. She dyes her special fibers
with natural materials like fustic and logwood,
creating gentle shades that we really love.

## KNITTED MEASUREMENTS

Circumference: Approx 18½" [47 cm]

## SIZES

To fit head sizes 20–22" [51–56 cm].
See Notes if you would like to change
size.

## MATERIALS

— Cormo Sport by Sincere Sheep
   [4 oz (114 g) skeins, each approx
   400 yds (366 m), 100% domestic
   Cormo wool]: 1 skein Mrs. Fisher,
   Epiphyte, or Cumulus
   *Note*: One skein is enough yarn to
   make 2 hats.
— Size US 3 (3.25 mm) circular needle,
   16" (40 cm)
— Size US 4 (3.5 mm) circular needle,
   16" (40 cm), or size needed to
   achieve gauge
— Size US 4 (3.5 mm) double-pointed
   needles (set of 6), or size needed to
   achieve gauge
— Stitch markers

## GAUGE

25 sts and 36 rnds = 4" (10 cm) over St st
(knit every rnd), using larger needle

## NOTES

This hat is worked in the round using
the spiral method. The marker is only
to count rounds—unless specified, the
sequence should be continued right past
the marker.

The patterns are changed by varying the
stitch count between 119, 120, and 121. In
the main sequence—[k5, p1, k3, p1]—the
pattern multiples are 10 stitches + 9, 10
stitches, and 10 stitches + 1, respectively,
and the pattern makes a left-leaning
swirl, ribbing, and a right-leaning swirl,
respectively.

The round repeat for the swirls is 10
rounds, so each swirl section will end
perfectly at the marker on the 10th round.

When working the crown, pull the yarn
firmly between the needles to minimize
laddering.

To increase or decrease the hat size,
change the stitch count in multiples of 10.

## HAT

Using smaller needle, CO 120 sts. Join, being careful not to twist sts; pm for beginning of rnd.

### FINE RIBBING

Work [k1, p1] for 3 rnds.

### PATTERNED RIBBING

Work [k5, p1, k3, p1] for 7 rnds.
Change to larger needle.

### STOCKINETTE

— *Rnds 1 and 2:* Knit.
— *Rnd 3:* Knit to last st, kfb—121 sts.

### RIGHT-LEANING SWIRL

Work [k5, p1, k3, p1] for 10 rnds.
Sequence will end perfectly at the end of the 10th rnd.

### STOCKINETTE

— *Rnd 1:* K2tog, knit to end—120 sts.
— *Rnd 2:* Knit.
— *Rnd 3:* Knit to last 2 sts, k2tog—119 sts.

### SWIRL HAT AT A GLANCE

(not including crown shaping)

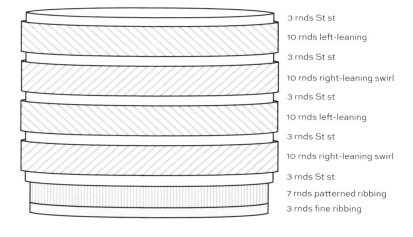

3 rnds St st

10 rnds left-leaning

3 rnds St st

10 rnds right-leaning swirl

3 rnds St st

10 rnds left-leaning

3 rnds St st

10 rnds right-leaning swirl

3 rnds St st

7 rnds patterned ribbing

3 rnds fine ribbing

## LEFT-LEANING SWIRL

Work [k5, p1, k3, p1] for 10 rnds. Sequence will end perfectly at the end of the 10th rnd.

## STOCKINETTE

— *Rnd 1:* Kfb, knit to end—120 sts.
— *Rnd 2:* Knit.
— *Rnd 3:* Knit to last st, kfb—121 sts.

## RIGHT-LEANING SWIRL

Work [k5, p1, k3, p1] for 10 rnds. Sequence will end perfectly at the end of the 10th rnd.

## STOCKINETTE

— *Rnd 1:* K2tog, knit to end—120 sts.
— *Rnd 2:* Knit.
— *Rnd 3:* Knit to last 2 sts, k2tog—119 sts.

## LEFT-LEANING SWIRL

Work [k5, p1, k3, p1] for 10 rnds. Sequence will end perfectly at the end of the 10th rnd.

## STOCKINETTE

— *Rnd 1:* Kfb, knit to end—120 sts.
— *Rnds 2 and 3:* Knit.

## CROWN

— Divide sts evenly onto 5 dpns, with 24 sts per dpn.
— *Dec Rnd:* [Knit to last 2 sts of needle, k2tog] 5 times—5 sts dec.
— Rep Dec Rnd until 10 sts remain. Cut yarn, thread tail through remaining sts, pull tight and fasten off.

## FINISHING

Weave in ends, wash, and block.

# FREAK FLAGS

**I**F YOU ARE ONE OF THOSE KNITTERS who thinks knitting always must serve a vital practical purpose, this may be a stretch for you.

This project is purely about the pleasure of knitting up a bunch of triangles in different sequence-knitting patterns. These pennants or banners (or, as we lovingly refer to them, freak flags) let you see how sequence knitting behaves when increases or decreases are in the mix—and they provide the pleasure of knitting with hand-dyed yarn.

When we discovered Amy Lee Serradell's Canon Hand Dyes at a fiber festival, we knew we had to match her artful mini-skeins with a project that allows maximum playfulness with color.

At the end of this joyful exercise, instead of a pile of swatches, you'll have a neatly joined ribbon of triangles that can brighten a corner of your home, a celebration, a Christmas mantel, or your very own neck. (Try it on before you make fun.)

## KNITTED MEASUREMENTS

Triangles: 6" [15 cm] along each edge

## BUNTING/SCARF

Width: 36" [91.5 cm] per 7 triangles
Length: 5" [12.5 cm]

## MATERIALS

— Charles Merino by Canon Hand
Dyes [25 g mini-skeins, each approx
100 yds (91.5 m), 80% merino wool/
20% nylon]: 1 mini-skein in each of
7 colors (indicated as A–G)
Colorway 1: Sunlight
Colorway 2: Candlelight
*Note*: One set of 7 mini-skeins is
enough for at least 14 triangles.
— One pair size US 3 (3.25 mm)
needles, or size needed to achieve
gauge
— Two size US 3 (3.25 mm) double-
pointed needles, for optional
I-cord tie

## GAUGE

Approx 28 sts and 32 rows = 4" (10 cm)
over St st

*Note*: Gauge will vary slightly from
triangle to triangle; it is not critical for
this project.

## NOTES

The pattern is written for a 7-triangle
bunting where each triangle is a different
stitch pattern and color. The bunting can
be made longer by repeating triangles
1–7 for a total of 14 triangles (as we did for
the bunting in our photos). Even longer is
possible—just add more triangles.

An optional 3-stitch I-cord can be added
at beginning and end for hanging. Work
I-cord to 10" (25.5 cm) or desired length,
then begin Triangle 1 with Sequence Row.
On the last triangle, BO until 3 sts remain
and then work the I-cord to the same
length as in the beginning.

On most rows you will not be able to work
a complete sequence before working the
increase at the end of the row. In the case
of a partial sequence, continue to work
leftover stitches in pattern to last stitch.

The tension along the diagonal edges
must be loose or the triangles will pucker.
Pulling more yarn through the first stitch
of every row helps.

Even though the bunting is made up of
6" (15 cm) triangles, the width is shorter
because the triangles overlap.

# TRIANGLE 1

*Working Optional I-Cord Tie*
— With A and DPNs, cast on 3 sts. *Do not turn; slide sts back to right-hand end of needle. Drawing yarn across back of knitting, k3; rep from * until I-cord measures approx 10" (25.5 cm). Proceed to Sequence Row.

*Working without I-Cord Tie*
— With A, make a slipknot and place on needle.
— *Set-Up Row 1:* Kbf—2 sts.
— *Set-Up Row 2:* K1, kbf—3 sts.
— *Sequence Row:* [K1, p1] to last st, kbf—1 st inc.
— Rep Sequence Row until you have 42 sts. BO until only 6 sts remain (including st on right-hand needle after BO), taking care to keep sts loose enough so triangle does not pucker. Slip st from right-hand needle back to left-hand needle. Cut A; do not turn work.

*The top 2 rows of bunting in this photo are Colorway 1/ Sunlight. The bottom 2 rows are Colorway 2/Candlelight.*

## TRIANGLE 2

- Continue across remaining 6 sts from previous triangle.
- *Sequence Row:* With B, [k2, p1] to last st, kbf—1 st inc.
- Rep Sequence Row until you have 42 sts. BO until only 6 sts remain (including st on right-hand needle after BO), taking care to keep sts loose enough so triangle does not pucker. Cut yarn; do not turn work.

## TRIANGLE 3

- *Sequence Row:* With C, [k2, p2] to last st, kbf—1 st inc.
- Complete as for Triangle 2.

## TRIANGLE 4

- *Sequence Row:* With D, [k3, p1] to last st, kbf—1 st inc.
- Complete as for Triangle 2.

## TRIANGLE 5

- *Sequence Row:* With E, [k3, p3] to last st, kbf—1 st inc.
- Complete as for Triangle 2.

## TRIANGLE 6

- *Sequence Row:* With F, [k4, p2] to last st, kbf—1 st inc.
- Complete as for Triangle 2.

## TRIANGLE 7

- *Sequence Row:* With G, [k5, p1] to last st, kbf—1 st inc.
- Rep Sequence Row until you have 42 sts. BO all sts, taking care to keep sts loose enough so triangle is not puckered. NOTE: If you prefer to work an optional I-cord tie, BO until 3 sts remain (including st on right-hand needle after BO), then work I-cord as for beginning of Bunting.

## FINISHING

Weave in ends, wash, and block each triangle to approx 6" (15 cm) along each edge, making sure to block to sharp points; trim ends flush.

*Left: The yarns in Colorway 1/ Sunlight are on the gold plates. The yarns in Colorway 2/ Candlelight are on the pewter plates.*

# PARALLELOGRAM
# SCARF

For once, we're celebrating bias. Beautiful, slanted bias. The wonderful bias that happens when you think you're knitting in one direction but discover things are not what they first appeared to be.

This scarf is worked on the bias with two different long-repeat yarns to create a soft, reversible, textured fabric. Every row is worked the same except for a double increase or double decrease every other row. The way you combine the yarns, for example, whether you work from the inside or the outside of the ball, affects the result in the most intriguing of fashions.

## KNITTED MEASUREMENTS
Width: Approx 8" [20.5 cm]
Length: Approx 70" [178 cm]

## MATERIALS
— Ombré Fingering Shawl Balls by
  Freia Fine Handpaints [3.53 oz balls,
  each approx 430 yds (393 m),
  100% US merino wool]
  Lichen-Vintage Colorway
  A: Lichen, 1 ball
  B: Vintage, 1 ball
  Cloud-Mist Colorway
  A: Cloud, 1 ball
  B: Mist, 1 ball
  Purpleheart-Whisper Colorway
  A: Purpleheart, 1 ball
  B: Whisper, 1 ball
— One pair size 5 (3.75 mm) needles,
  or size needed to achieve gauge
— Removable stitch markers

## GAUGE
23 sts and 43 rows = 4" (10 cm) over
scarf pattern

Note: To work a gauge swatch, CO a
multiple of 4 sts + 1 (a CO of 29 sts is
recommended), then repeat [k2, p2]
sequence to desired length.

## NOTES
See right to learn about the exciting
possibilities for color play when working
with long-repeat yarns.

Because the scarf is worked on the
bias, the cast-on is much longer than
expected. For the scarf to hang properly
with nice points, the tension of the
cast-on, bind-off, and sides is important.
Consider beginning with waste yarn and
a provisional cast-on, then changing to
your working yarn, leaving a tail 3 times
the width of the stitches on the needle.
After a few inches of the piece are complete, you can remove the provisional
cast-on and use the tail to bind off the
cast-on stitches.

The pattern multiple is 4 stitches + 1. The
width of the scarf can be adjusted by
increasing or decreasing the stitch count
in multiples of 4.

Every row is created by repeating the
sequence [k2, p2]. The only difference
from row to row is that odd-numbered
rows end with a double increase and
even-numbered rows end with a double
decrease.

## WORKING WITH LONG-REPEAT BALLS OF YARN

Working simultaneously with two long-repeat balls like the ones from Freia fibers is entertaining because the color play between the balls evolves with the knitting. The repeats are so long they can extend across an entire ball, and the choice for the start has a big effect on the final look. To make Parallelogram Scarves that look like ours, the color progression of your balls needs to match ours. If it does, begin from the outsides of the balls as shown below, and alternate the ball you work from every 2 rows. If the colors of your balls evolve in the reverse direction, pull from the middle or rewind the ball.

Color A: Lichen
Color B: Vintage

Color A: Cloud
Color B: Mist

Color A: Purpleheart
Color B: Whisper

You will not always be able to work a complete sequence before the end of the row. In the case of a partial sequence, continue to work the leftover stitches in pattern to the end.

The tension along the diagonal edges must be loose enough that it does not distort the drape. This is especially important on the edge where the yarns are swapped because the old yarn has to travel a long distance. When working the first stitch of a new row, pull through more yarn than you would normally. When changing colors, bring the new yarn up and to the right of the yarn just used to twist the yarns and prevent leaving a hole.

Markers help in the beginning to identify the increase and decrease sides. These markers, and markers added just before the bind-off, also help with blocking to sharp points.

## SCARF

With A, CO 101 sts. Place a removable marker around the first st (st near the working yarn) and 2 markers around the last st. The single marker indicates the decrease edge; the double marker indicates the increase edge. This can be helpful during the first inch of work.

— *Row 1:* [K2, p2] to last st, kbfb—103 sts.
— *Row 2:* [K2, p2] to last 3 sts, k3tog—101 sts.
— *Row 3:* With A, work first 3 sts (k2, p1), join B and beg with p1, work in pattern to last st, kbfb—103 sts.
— *Row 4:* Rep Row 2.
— *Row 5:* With B, work first 3 sts (k2, p1), with A and beg with p1, work in pattern to last st, kbfb—103 sts.
— *Row 6:* Rep Row 2.

Alternate A and B every 2 rows, taking great care with the tension of the first st, and especially the first st of a color-change row. Continue in this manner until yarn is almost consumed, leaving enough yarn to BO. On the last row, place a marker around the first and last sts to aid in blocking to sharp points. BO with special care to not distort the points.

## FINISHING

Weave ends into a section of the same color; trim ends to approximately 1" (2.5 cm). Soak in soapy water for at least 30 minutes, then rinse well and press or spin out water. Pin to final dimensions and let dry. Trim ends flush.

*When we combine sequence knitting and the glories of a slow-shifting gradient yarn, we land on knitting that is pure fun.*

*Colorways from top to bottom: Purpleheart-Whisper; Lichen-
Vintage; and Cloud-Mist*

# The Joy of Improv

I SAT DOWN WITH A PILE of Lamb's Pride Brown Sheep Worsted, one of the great blanket yarns, and spent a week in wild, unfettered sequence knitting glory. The notion of serpentine sequences is what got me. It requires virtually no planning. You work a sequence, and when you get to the end of the row, you continue it on the new row without interruption. It's a serpent, winding its way from front side to back side, across a flat fabric.

It is awesome. It creates fabrics that would never appear in a typical stitch dictionary—sometimes a serpentine sequence can run for 18 rows before it repeats.

I began a log cabin blanket, applying just a couple of rules: Every patch had to be 3" (7.5 cm) high. And I was not allowed to study any pictures of sequence swatches—I wanted my adventure in serpentine sequences to be as spontaneous as possible. I cast on 20 stitches and let fate determine the rest.

The result? The beginnings of a blanket that I made without having to do anything except follow Cecelia's fundamental recipe for knits and purls, worked continuously, without interruption at the end of a row. Patch 1: k3, p1; Patch 2: p4, k3; Patch 3: k2, p5; on and on I went, working each patch in a different sequence. At times, I fiddled with the number of rows to keep the patches all the same height. And I paid attention when picking up stitches for a new patch to try to keep all the patches the same width. Beyond that, it was pure, unfettered improv.

—Ann

SEQUENCE KNITTING

SIMPLE METHODS FOR CREATING COMPLEX FABRICS

## GETTING TO KNOW DESIGNER CECELIA CAMPOCHIARO

*Cecelia Campochiaro lives and works in Silicon Valley, where she develops specialized microscopes used in computer chip manufacturing. The arts have been a lifelong passion running parallel to her technical life. She had an Aha! knitting moment in 2010, when she realized that textured fabrics could be created by the simple repetition of a sequence of stitches.*

*This Field Guide is only an introduction to the world of sequence knitting. We encourage you to climb on board the mothership and*

*get yourself a copy of Cecelia's extraordinary book,* Sequence Knitting. *It is so rich, such a deep exploration of an idea—and one of the most beautiful knitting books we've ever seen.*

*We are humbled and delighted to have had the opportunity to work with Cecelia.*

**What has surprised you the most during your sequence knitting odyssey?**
My biggest surprise has been the warm welcome from so many knitters and contributors to the fiber world. It is a daunting experience to self-publish a book, and I was not sure how it would be received. Making new friends who share my passion for textiles, design, and knitting has been a joy.

**What advice do you have for a newcomer to this sort of knitting?**
Understand that sequence knitting is a mindset shift. It can be done in a range of difficulty from very easy 1-row patterns to hard-to-read serpentine patterns. Regardless of the pattern, having a way to know you are on track is important, e.g., knowing that a sequence must end evenly after 4 rows or something is wrong. I tell everyone to start a project

by making a swatch that is at least 3 inches high. After 3 inches, you can see the pattern build up; you'll have confidence in how it looks and how the knitting works, and you'll know if you are comfortable with that sequence being repeated again and again in your head like an earworm.

**How do you juggle your full-time day job in technology with designing, teaching, and writing books in the knitting world?**
I try to use the edges around my work schedule for knitting. There is often one good truly silent hour in the early morning, maybe another 30 to 60 minutes in the early evening, plus larger blocks of time on weekends and when I extend the weekend with a day or two of paid time off.

**Do you ever need to take the day off from all of it?**
Sometimes I need puttering days. On these days I don't think about high-tech or knitting, and I get caught up on errands or chores. I also like to go to museums to be inspired. My home is about an hour south of San Francisco, where we have some great museums, and my vacations always feature museum visits. Some recent memorable exhibits include Diebenkorn & Matisse at SFMOMA, Vilhelm Lundstrøm at the Brandts in Odense, Denmark, and Commes des Garçons at the Met in New York.

**How on earth did you create the hundreds of swatches for your book?**
Two sample knitters made all the swatches. One of them has continued to knit swatches for me for future books. Sometimes I think a fabric will be great and the swatch is meh, and sometimes I am amazed by a swatch. I love swatching now; ten years ago I saw it as a waste.

**Who are your knitting heroes?**
There are many knitters and designers I love and admire, but Elizabeth Zimmermann is my biggest hero. I wish I had been able to meet her.

**Security Question (We'd like to get into your PayPal account if that's OK)—What was the first concert you ever attended?**
Queen. I was 11 and had a crush on Freddie Mercury. My Dad took me and some friends.

## ABBREVIATIONS

[ ]: *Instructions within brackets will be repeated across the row/round. You may have a partial sequence at the end of a row; any remaining stitches at the end of any row should fit as much of the sequence as possible.*

| | |
|---|---|
| **Approx:** | Approximately |
| **Beg:** | Begin(ning)(s) |
| **BO:** | Bind off |
| **CO:** | Cast on |
| **Dec:** | Decreas(ed)(es)(ing) |
| **Dpn:** | Double-pointed needle(s) |
| **Inc:** | Increas(ed)(es)(ing) |
| **Kbf:** | Knit into the back and front of the next stitch. |
| **Kfb:** | Knit into the front and back of the next stitch. |
| **Kbfb:** | Knit into the back, front, then back of the next stitch. |
| **K2tog:** | Knit 2 stitches together. |
| **K:** | Knit |
| **Pm:** | Place marker |
| **P:** | Purl |
| **Rep:** | Repeat(ed)(ing)(s) |
| **Rev St st:** | reverse Stockinette stitch |
| **Rnd(s):** | Round(s) |
| **RS:** | Right side |
| **St st:** | Stockinette stitch |
| **St(s):** | Stitch(es) |
| **Tog:** | Together |
| **WS:** | Wrong side |

# AN INVITATION

*Perhaps this is your first Mason-Dixon Knitting Field Guide. Maybe you've collected them all. If you've found this guidebook, we're going to guess that you're a daily knitter, or a regular knitter. Certainly, you are a knitter who is curious, attractive, and a generally above-average sort of person.*

- Our website, Mason-Dixon Knitting, is created for you, the curious knitter.

- We bring you new stories and discoveries and treasures every day of the week, with contributors who are the greatest talents in the knitting world.

- We believe that knitting is part of a life well lived, so we cover a lot of ground—personal style, self-care, food, and our recommendations for podcasts and binge-worthy TV.

- When you visit MDK regularly, you will develop an excellent knowledge of what's beautiful and amazing in the world of knitting.

- The MDK forum, called the Lounge, is our virtual hangout, where you will find like-minded knitters who never seem to knit enough.

- Thousands of knitters have discovered that the MDK Shop is the source of special, hard-to-find yarns. These yarns, including the yarns featured in this Field Guide, have been chosen with care and are often exclusive to MDK.

- We spend a lot of time creating all of this for you, because we know you're as nuts for knitting as we are. We hope you'll come visit MasonDixonKnitting.com every day. There's so much to see.